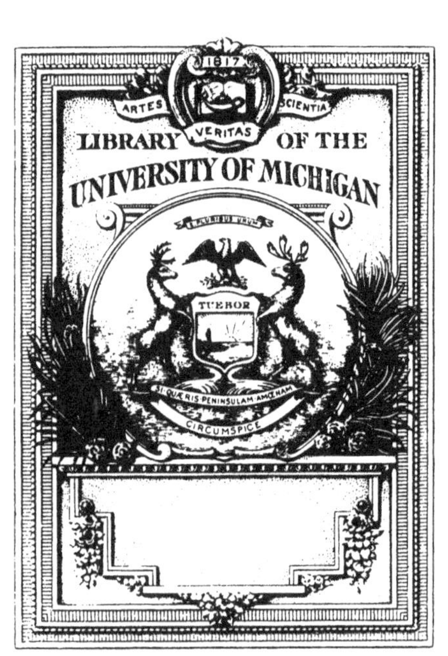
1817
ARTES
VERITAS
SCIENTIA
LIBRARY OF THE
UNIVERSITY OF MICHIGAN
TUEBOR
SI QUÆRIS PENINSULAM AMŒNAM
CIRCUMSPICE

RULES AND PROCEDURE

ADOPTED BY

The Parole Commission

OF

THE CITY OF NEW YORK

RULES AND PROCEDURE

ADOPTED BY

The Parole Commission

OF

THE CITY OF NEW YORK

BERTRAM de N. CRUGER,
Chairman,

HARRY STACKELL,

JOHN C. MAHER,

FREDERICK A. WALLIS, *ex-officio,*

RICHARD E. ENRIGHT, *ex-officio,*

THOMAS R. MINNICK,
Secretary.

RULES OF ORDER

GOVERNING THE

PAROLE COMMISSION OF THE CITY OF NEW YORK

Rule 1. The Officers of the Commission shall consist of a Chairman and a Secretary.

Rule 2. A majority of the members of the Commission shall constitute a quorum for the transaction of business. No business shall be transacted without the actual presence of three or more members.

Rule 3. In the absence of the Chairman, the Commission shall elect an Acting Chairman, who shall perform all the duties of the Chairman.

Rule 4. It shall be the duty of the Chairman, appointed by the Mayor, or the Acting Chairman, to preside at all meetings of the Commission and to perform such other duties from time to time as the Commission may direct.

Rule 5. The duties of the Secretary of the Commission shall be to keep a full set of the minutes of each meeting of the Commission, and keep a list of inmates subject to parole, and their records; to report to the Commission all communications and all official action taken between the meetings; notify the magistrates and judges making commitments of persons whose cases are to come before the Commission for parole, in accordance with Section 3 of the parole law; notify the Commissioner of Correction and the proper Wardens of the action taken by the Parole Commission; and to transact such other business as may be delegated to him from time to time by the Commission.

Rule 6. Regular meetings of the Commission shall be held (except in the months of July and August, for which months other provision shall be made according to necessity) on each Thursday of the week, at 10 A. M., provided that when said day shall fall upon a legal holiday, such meeting shall be held upon another day to be designated by the Parole Commission at the preceding regular meeting.

Rule 7. Special meetings of the Commission may be called by the Chairman, or, in his absence, by the Secretary, upon the request, in writing, of two members, but notice of the same shall be sent to the addresses of each member of the Commission at least twenty-four hours before the time for which such meeting is called, and shall state the object of the meeting. No other business shall be transacted at such meeting except with the unanimous consent of the full board. The members of the Parole Commission shall file with the Secretary, addresses to which such notices may be sent; and a letter addressed and mailed in accordance therewith shall be due notice.

Rule 8. The regular order of business at the meetings of the Commission shall be as follows:

1. Roll Call.
2. Action on minutes of the previous meeting.
3. Communications.
4. Report of the Committees in order of appointment.
5. Report of Parole Officers.
6. Action on the reports in their regular order.
7. Unfinished business.
8. Consideration and determination of minimum periods of imprisonment before eligibility for parole.
9. The granting of paroles and discharges.
10. New business.

Rule 9. On all questions, except where the vote is unanimous, the Commissioners shall vote as their names are called by the Secretary, and the vote of each member shall be recorded in the minutes. The names of the appointed members shall be called first, and the names of the ex-officio members shall be called thereafter.

Rule 10. Where the vote is not unanimous, every member of the Commission who shall be present when the question is put, shall vote for or against the same, unless excused by the Commission.

Rule 11. A majority of the whole Commission shall be required to appoint or remove any Secretary, Clerk, Parole Officer or other employee of the Commission. No Clerk, Secretary or other employee of the Commission shall be removed except at a regular meeting of the Commission and upon five days previous notice in writing served upon him, specifying the cause of his proposed removal, and that he be given an opportunity for an explanation in the presence of the Commission, and in accordance with the Civil Service Law.

Rule 12. In accordance with the provisions of Section 3 of the Parole Law, this Commission shall locate and maintain a central office in the Borough of Brooklyn. It shall assign one of its Parole Officers to be assistant in charge of said office and such additional officers and clerical force from time to time as the business of the office may require. To avoid unnecessary expense and to better preserve close contact between Parole Officers and Parole Commissioners, it was decided to establish a number of places in Brooklyn in accordance with territorial needs, where paroled inmates could meet their respective officers.

Rule 13. The officers of the Parole Commission shall be open daily, Sundays and legal holidays excepted, from 9 A. M. to 5 P. M., except on Saturdays, when the office may close at 12 M., unless otherwise specified by public authorities.

Rule 14. These rules, and any additional rules adopted by this Commission, may, from time to time, be amended at any regular meeting of the Commission by a vote of three members of the Commission, provided that at least two weeks notice shall have been given at a preceding regular meeting; except that the number to constitute a quorum for the transaction of business may not be reduced.

Rule 15. The sessions of the Parole Commission, as provided for in the above rules, shall be executive in character and no person shall attend except the Commissioners, the Secretary and the official stenographer, unless the presence of another person or persons is secured by subpoena or request of the Commission.

RULES OF PROCEDURE FOR ESTABLISHING THE ELIGIBILITY FOR PAROLE OF ALL INMATES COMMITTED TO THE CITY REFORMATORY, PENITENTIARY AND WORKHOUSE.

1. Interviewing of Inmates.

As soon as practicable after the admission of a prisoner over whom the Parole Commission obtains jurisdiction a member of the Parole Commission shall interview the inmate and shall examine court reports, police reports, reports of probation and parole officers, the original interview sheet, the medical report, and such other reports as the case may require; thereupon he shall recommend at a regular meeting of the Parole Commission a disposition of the case, which will be acted upon by vote of the assembled Commission.

2. Periods of Detention.

1. When an inmate is committed to the City Workhouse the Commission shall fix a period of confinement in years, months or days.

Penitentiary and Reformatory.

2. The Commission shall allot a number of marks to each inmate, the date of parole of such inmate being dependent upon his or her conduct and industry and the consequent rate at which he or she earns the marks allotted.

3. The case of each individual who has either earned the number of merit marks required for consideration, or who shall have served the fixed time allotted by the Commission, shall come up at a meeting of the Parole Commission during the month preceding the date on which such marks shall have been earned. The Commission shall consider, in addition to the earning of the number of merit marks or the serving of the fixed sentence, the Resident Physician's certificate stating the condition of health of inmate, and also a reasonable prospect of work and a suitable home being provided for the inmate upon his or her release.

Parole Violators.

4. A paroled inmate may be returned to custody for violation of parole upon a warrant executed by a member of the Commission, either with or without interviewing the offending inmate.

Before the period of confinement of such violators shall be fixed, a Parole Commissioner shall interview the inmate and examine the reports and records of the case in the same manner as is done in the case of the original offender.

5. The above rules shall not be interpreted so as to prevent the Commission from giving consideration to any special case which may be brought to its attention upon the presentation of new facts by a member or Secretary of the Commission, but no action shall be taken without considering the conduct of the inmate as evidenced by reports of infractions, if any, and penalties inflicted therefor. Such reports to be furnished to this Commission by the Commissioner of Correction as they occur from time to time.

6. All inquiries and communications by the Parole Commission relative to inmates in the custody of the Department of Correction shall be addressed to the Commissioner of Correction.

7. All existing rules and resolutions inconsistent with the above are hereby abolished and rescinded.

LOCAL—NEW YORK, KINGS, QUEENS, RICHMOND, BRONX, ERIE AND MONROE COUNTIES

[Twenty-four folios.]

LAWS OF NEW YORK—By Authority

Chapter 579

AN ACT extending and developing the reformatory and correctional functions of workhouses, penitentiaries and reformatories under the jurisdiction of departments of correction in cities of the first class, providing for the sentence, commitment, parole, conditional discharge and reapprehension of persons committed to such institutions and for the establishment of a parole commission in such cities.

Became a law May 10, 1915, with the approval of the Governor. Passed three-fifths being present.

Submitted to the Cities of New York, Buffalo and Rochester and accepted by same.

The People of the State of New York, represented in Senate and Assembly, do enact as follows:

Section 1. The board of estimate and apportionment or other corresponding board or body in any city of the first class wherein there is a department of correction having jurisdiction over a workhouse, a penitentiary and a reformatory, is hereby authorized and empowered to provide by resolution for the creation of a parole commission, to be constituted and appointed and to possess the powers and be subject to the duties as hereinafter specified.

§ 2. In the event of such action by the board of estimate and apportionment or other corresponding board or body as aforesaid, then within sixty days thereafter the mayor of such city shall appoint three members of the said commission who, together with the commissioner of correction, ex-officio, and the police commissioner, ex-officio, of said city shall constitute the parole commission in and for said city. Of the three appointive members first named hereunder, one shall hold office for two years, one for four years and one for six years, as shall be designated by the mayor. Upon the expiration of each of said terms the mayor shall appoint a successor for the full term of ten years. Vacancies occurring by expiration of a term shall be filled by the mayor for the full term; vacancies occurring from any other cause shall be filled by the mayor for the unexpired term only. Any of the appointive members of said commission shall be subject to removal by the mayor on account of official misconduct or neglect of official duty, or mental or physical inability to perform his official duties, but before such removal the member shall be entitled to due and timely notice in writing of the charges against him and to a copy thereof, and to a public hearing on like notice before the mayor. The board of estimate and apportionment or other corresponding board, boards or body having jurisdiction thereof, shall determine whether or not the appointive members of the commission shall receive any compensation for their services and the amount thereof. But neither the commissioner of correction nor the police commissioner as ex-officio members of such commission shall receive any compensation as such. Each of the appointive members of the commission shall before entering upon the duties of his office take the oath of office prescribed by the constitution of the state.

§ 3. The commissioner of correction of any of said cities shall be the president of the parole commission of such city. A majority of the members of the commission shall constitute a quorum for the transaction of business. It shall be the duty of said commission to meet at least once in each week, except during the months of July and August. If by reason of pressure of official business or otherwise, the commissioner of correction or the police commissioner shall deem his absence from a meeting of the parole commission necessary, he may designate a deputy commissioner to represent him, and such deputy commissioners shall possess all the power and perform all the duties of said commissioners, respectively, as members of the said parole commission. The parole commission in and for the city of New York shall maintain a central office in the borough of Manhattan and a central office in the borough of Brooklyn. Any committing magistrate or judge of any court who shall make commitments under indeterminate sentence to a workhouse or a reformatory under the jurisdiction of a department of correction, as provided in this act, shall be entitled to sit with parole commission of said city during the consideration of the eligibility for parole of any person by him committed to any such institution under an indeterminate sentence, with authority to vote on such matter. The parole commission shall give or cause to be given due notice to each of such committing magistrates or judges, stating the time and place of the meeting of the commission and the names, offenses, dates of commitment and the recommendations of the parole officers and officers of the department of correction of all inmates committed by him to a workhouse or reformatory under indeterminate sentences whose eligibility for parole is to be considered at the next meeting of the commission. The parole commission shall, so far as practicable, regard the convenience of said magistrates and judges in arranging its meetings for the consideration of the eligibility of persons for parole and in placing such cases upon its calendar for consideration.

§ 4. After the creation of a parole commission in any of the said cities as hereinbefore provided, any person convicted of any offense punishable by imprisonment in a penitentiary, workhouse, city prison, county jail or other institution under the jurisdiction of the department of correction of said city, who shall not be committed in default of payment of a fine imposed, or for failure to furnish surety or sureties upon a conviction of disorderly conduct tending to a breach of the peace, or for abandonment, and who is not insane or mentally or physically incapable of being substantially benefited by the correctional and reformatory purposes of any such institutions shall, if committed to any institution under the jurisdiction of the department of correction in said city, be sentenced and committed to a penitentiary or a workhouse or a reformatory under the jurisdiction of the said department of correction. The duration of the commitment of any person to the penitentiary shall not be fixed or limited by the court in imposing sentence, except that the term of such imprisonment in said institution shall not exceed three years, and such imprisonment shall be terminated as prescribed in section five of this act. The duration of the commitment of any person to a workhouse shall be for a definite period not to exceed six months, provided, however, that if it shall become known to the court through competent evidence at any stage of the proceeding prior to the imposition of sentence that any person convicted of vagrancy, disorderly conduct tending to a breach of the peace, public prostitution, soliciting on streets or public places for the purposes of prostitution, or frequenting disorderly houses, or a house of prostitution, or the violation of section one hundred and fifty of chapter ninety-nine of the laws of nineteen hundred and nine, as amended, has been convicted of any or each of these offenses two or more times during the twenty-four months just previous, or three or more times previous to that conviction, then the court shall commit such offender to a workhouse, of the said department of correction in said city for an indeterminate period which shall not exceed two years. The term of such imprisonment of any person so convicted and sentenced to a workhouse shall be terminated by the parole commission as prescribed in this act. Commitment to reformatories for male misdemeanants under the jurisdiction of a department of correction in any of the cities as aforesaid shall be made in conformity with laws providing for such institutions and commitments thereto. The term of imprisonment of persons so convicted and sentenced to reformatories shall be terminated by the parole commission as prescribed in this act.

§ 5. The parole commission shall have power to parole, conditionally release, discharge, retake or reimprison without reference to the committing magistrate or judge, except as provided in section three of this act, any inmate of any workhouse or reformatory under the jurisdiction of the department of correction in said city, committed thereto under an indeterminate sentence; and to parole, conditionally release, discharge, retake or reimprison any inmate of any penitentiary under the jurisdiction of a department of correction in said cities, committed thereto under an indeterminate sentence, provided the judge who made such commitment to such penitentiary shall, upon recommendation of the parole commission created in pursuance of this act, approve in writing such parole, conditional release or discharge of such inmate. The said commission shall have power to make all necessary rules and regulations not inconsistent with the laws of the State, prescribing the conditions under which eligibility for parole may be determined and under which inmates may be paroled, conditionally released, discharged, retaken and reimprisoned. The said commission shall have full power to compel the attendance of witnesses; to administer oaths; to examine such persons as may be necessary or expedient; to investigate or cause to be investigated the record, health, ability and character previous to commitment and during imprisonment of each inmate committed under an indeterminate sentence to any penitentiary, workhouse or reformatory of the department of correction in said city. It shall also be the duty of the said commission to facilitate the establishment of a uniform system of records, reports, statistics and memoranda treating of persons charged with or convicted of crimes and offenses punishable by imprisonment in any of the correctional institutions of a department of correction of said city, and to make recommendations from time to time to the courts having criminal jurisdiction therein.

§ 6. The appointment and qualification of the members of the parole commission in any of the cities as aforesaid shall abolish any existing board of parole, body or agent authorized to regulate the parole, discharge or reimprisonment of any person or persons committed under an indeterminate sentence to any institution under the jurisdiction of the department of correction of said city, and any board of parole, body or agent so abolished shall immediately deliver to such parole commission in said city, all papers, documents, records and other memoranda in its possession relating to inmates theretofore so committed, and jurisdiction over such inmates shall thereupon vest in such parole commission in accordance with the provisions of this act. All persons in the employ of any such board of parole, body or agent as aforesaid, on the first day of January, nineteen hundred and fifteen, in a position appearing in the competitive class of the civil service classification of the municipal civil service commission of said city or of the state civil service commission and still so employed at the time of the abolishment of such board of parole, body or agent as provided in this act, shall be transferred to and employed at the same rate of compensation by the superseding parole commission, and such persons shall perform such duties as directed by said parole commission. Upon the creation in any of said cities of a parole commission in pursuance of this act, the parole officers, superintendents, overseers, wardens, deputy wardens, instructors, head keepers, keepers, foremen of stables and drivers of the department of corrections in said city shall be and become peace officers within the provisions of section one hundred and fifty-four of the code of criminal procedure.

§ 7. For the purpose of reformatory and correctional treatment of persons committed to a department of correction in any of said cities, the commissioner of correction of such city shall have power to transfer inmates from any institution of the department to any other institution of the department; but nothing in this act shall be construed as empowering the said parole commission of any of said cities to control, manage or supervise, in any manner whatsoever, any of the institutions under the jurisdiction of the department of correction therein. It shall be lawful for the several boards of supervisors in the several counties of this state to enter into agreements with the board of estimate and apportionment or other corresponding board or body of any of the said cities wherein there shall be established a parole commission as provided in this act, to receive and keep in a workhouse or penitentiary under the jurisdiction of the department of correction of such city any person who may be sentenced to confinement therein by any court or magistrate in any of the said several counties of this state for any definite term not less than sixty days or more than one year.

§ 8. Nothing in this act shall be construed to prohibit any court of competent jurisdiction from placing on probation, or from suspending sentence upon any person convicted in that court, as provided by statute.

§ 9. Nothing in this act contained shall be deemed to affect or impair in any manner any provision of the penal laws or of the code of criminal procedure which relates to the sentence, commitment, parole, discharge or reimprisonment of any person committed to any institution other than those institutions specified in this act, the intent of this act being to empower magistrates and courts of or in cities of the first class, in the circumstances hereinbefore specified, to commit persons under indeterminate sentence to penitentiaries, reformatories and workhouses and to extend the reformatory and correctional functions of each and all of such institutions.

§ 10. This act shall take effect immediately.

STATE OF NEW YORK,
Office of the Secretary of State, } ss:

I have compared the preceding with the original law on file in this office, and do hereby certify that the same is a correct transcript therefrom and of the whole of said original law.

FRANCIS M. HUGO,
Secretary of State.

LOCAL—NEW YORK, KINGS, QUEENS, RICHMOND, BRONX, ERIE AND MONROE COUNTIES

[Twenty-five folios.]

LAWS OF NEW YORK—By Authority

Chapter 287

AN ACT to amend chapter five hundred and seventy-nine of the laws of nineteen hundred and fifteen, entitled " An act extending and developing the reformatory and correctional functions of workhouses, penitentiaries and reformatories under the jurisdiction of departments of correction in cities of the first class, providing for the sentence, commitment, parole, conditional discharge and reapprehension of persons committed to such institutions and for the establishment of a parole commission in such cities," generally.

Became a law April 24, 1916, with the approval of the Governor. Passed, three-fifths being present.

The People of the State of New York, represented in Senate and Assembly, do enact as follows:

Section 1. Section two of chapter five hundred and seventy-nine of the laws of nineteen hundred and fifteen, entitled "An act extending and developing the reformatory and correctional functions of workhouses, penitentiaries and reformatories under the jurisdiction of departments of correction in cities of the first class, providing for the sentence, commitment, parole, conditional discharge and reapprehension of persons committed to such institutions and for the establishment of a parole commission in such cities," is hereby amended to read as follows:

§ 2. In the event of such action by the board of estimate and apportionment or other corresponding board or body as aforesaid, then within sixty days thereafter the mayor of such city shall appoint three members of the said commission who, together with the commissioner of correction, ex-officio, and the police commissioner, ex-officio, of said city shall constitute the parole commission in and for said city. Of the three appointive members first named hereunder, one shall hold office for two years, one for four years and one for six years, as shall be designated by the mayor. Upon the expiration of each of said terms the mayor shall appoint a successor for the full term of ten years. Vacancies occurring by expiration of a term shall be filled by the mayor for the full term; vacancies occurring from any other cause shall be filled by the mayor for the unexpired term only. Any of the appointive members of said commission shall be subject to removal by the mayor on account of official misconduct or neglect of official duty, or mental or physical inability to perform his official duties, but before such removal the member shall be entitled to due and timely notice in writing of the charges against him and to a copy thereof, and to a public hearing on like notice before the mayor. The board of estimate and apportionment or other corresponding board, boards or body having jurisdiction thereof, shall determine whether or not the appointive members of the commission shall receive any compensation for their services and the amount thereof. But neither the commissioner of correction nor the police commissioner, as ex-officio members of such commission, shall receive any compensation as such. Each of the appointive members of the commission shall, before entering upon the duties of his office, take the oath of office prescribed by the constitution of the state. The mayor of any of said cities shall designate one of such members to be the chairman of the parole commission of such city, and may, at the expiration of the term of the member appointed to hold office for two years, designate the member appointed for four years, or the member appointed for six years, or the member then appointed for a full ten-year term, to be the chairman of the parole commission of such city.

§ 2. Section three of such chapter is hereby amended to read as follows:

§ 3. A majority of the members of the commission shall constitute a quorum for the transaction of business. It shall be the duty of said commission to meet at least once in each week, except during the months of July and August. If by reason of pressure of official business or otherwise, the commissioner of correction or the police commissioner shall deem his absence from a meeting of the parole commission necessary, he may designate a deputy commissioner to represent him, and such deputy commissioner shall possess all the powers and perform all the duties of said commissioners, respectively, as members of the parole commission. The parole commission in and for the city of New York shall maintain a central office in the borough of Manhattan and a central office in the borough of Brooklyn. Any committing magistrate or judge of any court who shall make commitments under indeterminate sentences to a workhouse or a reformatory under the jurisdiction of a department of correction, as provided in this act, shall be entitled to sit with the parole commission of said city during the consideration of the eligibility for parole of any person by him committed to any institution under an indeterminate sentence, with authority to vote on such matter. The parole commission shall give, or cause to be given, due notice to each of such committing magistrates or judges, stating the time and place of the meeting of the commission and the names, offenses, dates of commitment and the recommendations of the parole officers and officers of the department of correction of all inmates committed by him to a workhouse or reformatory under indeterminate sentences whose eligibility for parole is to be considered at the next meeting of the commission. The parole commission shall, so far as practicable, regard the convenience of said magistrates and judges in arranging its meetings for the consideration of the eligibility of persons for parole and in placing such cases upon its calendar for consideration.

§ 3. Section four of such chapter is hereby amended to read as follows:

§ 4. After the creation of a parole commission in any of the said cities, as hereinbefore provided, any person convicted of any crime or offense upon conviction for which the court may sentence to a penitentiary, workhouse, city prison, county jail or other institution under the jurisdiction of the department of correction of said city, who shall not be committed in default of payment of a fine imposed, or for failure to furnish surety or sureties upon a conviction of disorderly conduct tending to a breach of the peace or of abandonment, and who is not insane or mentally or physically incapable of being substantially benefited by the correctional and reformatory purposes of any such institution shall, if sentenced to any institution under the jurisdiction of the department of correction in said city, be sentenced and committed to a penitentiary or a workhouse or a reformatory under the jurisdiction of the said department of correction. No person shall be committed to a penitentiary under the jurisdiction of a department of correction in any such city because of failure to pay any fine or fines imposed, or for failure to furnish surety or sureties, or to a penitentiary, reformatory or workhouse under the jurisdiction of a department of correction in any such city for a term of imprisonment with a fine imposed in addition to the term of imprisonment. The term of imprisonment of any person sentenced to any such penitentiary shall not be fixed or limited by the court in imposing sentence. The term of such imprisonment shall be terminated in the manner prescribed in section five of this act and not otherwise, and shall not exceed three years. The term of imprisonment of any person sentenced to any such workhouse shall be fixed by the court in imposing sentence which term shall be for a definite period and shall not exceed six months; provided, however, that no person convicted in any of said cities of vagrancy, disorderly conduct tending to a breach of the peace, public prostitution, soliciting on streets or public places for the purpose of prostitution, or the violation of section one hundred and fifty of chapter ninety-nine of the laws of nineteen hundred and nine, as amended, shall be sentenced to any such workhouse for a definite term until the fingerprint records of the city magistrates' courts of said city are officially searched with reference to the particular defendant and the results thereof duly certified to the court; and provided, further, that if it shall appear to the court at any stage of the proceeding prior to the imposition of sentence and after due notice and opportunity to the defendant to be heard in opposition to such accusation of prior convictions that any person convicted of any or each of these offenses last enumerated has been convicted of any or each of these offenses two or more times during the twenty-four months just previous, or three or more times previous to that conviction, then the court shall sentence such offender to a workhouse of the said department of correction in said city for an indeterminate period. The term of imprisonment of any person convicted and sentenced to any such workhouse for an indeterminate period shall not exceed two years and shall be terminated by the parole commission in the manner prescribed in section five of this act and not otherwise. Commitment to reformatories for male misdemeanants under the jurisdiction of a department of correction in any of the cities as aforesaid shall be made in conformity with laws providing for such institutions and commitments thereto. The term of imprisonment of persons so convicted and sentenced to reformatories shall be terminated by the parole commission in the manner prescribed in section five of this act and not otherwise.

Nothing in this section shall be deemed to interfere with or prevent the commitment of any person in accordance with law to a state institution or to any other institution not under the jurisdiction of a department of correction in any of the said cities which was on May tenth, nineteen hundred and fifteen, or now is or may hereafter be authorized by law to receive persons convicted in the courts in any of said cities.

§ 4. Section five of such chapter is hereby amended to read as follows:

§ 5. The parole commission shall have power to parole, conditionally release, discharge, retake or reimprison without reference to the committing magistrate or judge, except as provided in section three of this act, any inmate of any workhouse or reformatory under the jurisdiction of the department of correction in said city, committed thereto under an indeterminate sentence; and to parole, conditionally release, discharge, retake or reimprison any inmate of any penitentiary under the jurisdiction of a department of correction in said cities, committed thereto under an indeterminate sentence, provided the judge or court who made such commitment to such penitentiary, or any successor thereof, shall, upon recommendation of the parole commission created in pursuance of this act, approve in writing such parole, conditional release or discharge of such inmate. The said commission shall have power to make all necessary rules and regulations not inconsistent with the laws of the state, prescribing the conditions under which eligibility for parole may be determined and under which inmates may be paroled, conditionally released, discharged, retaken and reimprisoned. The said commission and each and every member thereof shall have full power to compel the attendance of witnesses; to administer oaths; to examine such persons as may be necessary or expedient; to investigate or cause to be investigated the record, health, ability and character previous to commitment and during imprisonment of each inmate committed under an indeterminate sentence to any penitentiary, workhouse, or reformatory of the department of correction in said city. It shall also be the duty of the said commission to facilitate the establishment of a uniform system of records, reports, statistics and memoranda treating of persons charged with or convicted of crimes and offenses punishable by imprisonment in any of the correctional institutions of a department of correction of said city, and to make recommendations from time to time to the courts having criminal jurisdiction therein.

§ 5. Section six of such chapter is hereby amended to read as follows:

§ 6. The appointment and qualification of members of the parole commission in any of the cities as aforesaid shall abolish any existing board of parole, body or agent authorized to regulate the parole, discharge or reimprisonment of any person or persons committed under an indeterminate sentence to any institution under the jurisdiction of the department of correction of said city, and any board of parole, body or agent so abolished shall immediately deliver to such parole commission in said city, all papers, documents, records and other memoranda in its possession relating to inmates theretofore so committed, and jurisdiction over such inmates shall thereupon vest in such parole commission in accordance with the provisions of this act. All persons in the employ of any such board of parole, body or agent as aforesaid, on the first day of January, nineteen hundred and fifteen, in a position appearing in the competitive class of the civil service classification of the municipal civil service commission of said city or of the state civil service commission and still so employed at the time of the abolishment of such board of parole, body or agent as provided in this act, shall be transferred to and employed at the same rate of compensation by the superseding parole commission, and such persons shall perform such duties as directed by said parole commission. Upon the creation in any of said cities of a parole commission in pursuance of this act, the parole officers, superintendent, overseers, wardens, deputy wardens, instructors, head keepers, keepers, engineers, firemen, pilots, foremen of stables and drivers of the department of correction in said city shall be and become peace officers within the provisions of section one hundred and fifty-four of the code of criminal procedure.

§ 6. This act shall take effect immediately.

STATE OF NEW YORK,
Office of the Secretary of State, } ss:

I have compared the preceding with the original law on file in this office, and do hereby certify that the same is a correct transcript therefrom and of the whole of said original law.

FRANCIS M. HUGO,
Secretary of State.

[Seven folios.]

LAWS OF NEW YORK—By Authority

Chapter 242

AN ACT to amend chapter five hundred and seventy-nine of the laws of nineteen hundred and fifteen, entitled "An act extending and developing the reformatory and correctional functions of workhouses, penitentiaries and reformatories under the jurisdiction of departments of correction in cities of the first class, providing for the sentence, commitment, parole, conditional discharge and reapprehension of persons committed to such institutions and for the establishment of a parole commission in such cities," in relation to the appointive members of the commission.

Became a law April 15, 1919, with the approval of the Governor. Passed, three-fifths being present.

The People of the State of New York, represented in Senate and Assembly, do enact as follows:

Section 1. Section two of chapter five hundred and seventy-nine of the laws of nineteen hundred and fifteen, entitled "An act extending and developing the reformatory and correctional functions of workhouses, penitentiaries and reformatories under the jurisdiction of departments of correction in cities of the first class, providing for the sentence, commitment, parole, conditional discharge and reapprehension of persons committed to such institutions and for the establishment of a parole commission in such cities," as amended by chapter two hundred and eighty-seven of the laws of nineteen hundred and sixteen, is hereby amended to read as follows:

§ 2. In the event of such action by the board of estimate and apportionment or other corresponding board or body as aforesaid, then within sixty days thereafter the mayor of such city shall appoint three members of the said commission who, together with the commissioner of correction, ex-officio, and the police commissioner, ex-officio, of said city, shall constitute the parole commission in and for said city. Of the three appointive members first named hereunder, one shall hold office for two years, one for four years and one for six years, as shall be designated by the mayor. Upon the expiration of each of said terms the mayor shall appoint a successor for the full term of ten years. Vacancies occurring by expiration of a term shall be filled by the mayor for the full term; vacancies occurring from any other cause shall be filled by the mayor for the unexpired term only. Any of the appointive members of said commission shall be subject to removal by the mayor on account of official misconduct or neglect of official duty, or mental or physical inability to perform his official duties, but before such removal the member shall be entitled to due and timely notice in writing of the charges against him and to a copy thereof, and to a public hearing on like notice before the mayor. The board of estimate and apportionment or other corresponding board, boards or body having jurisdiction thereof, shall determine whether or not the appointive members of the commission shall receive any compensation for their services and the amount thereof. Such appointive members shall give full time to their work as members of the commission. But neither the commissioner of correction nor the police commissioner, as ex-officio members of such commission shall receive any compensation as such. Each of the appointive members of the commission shall before entering upon the duties of his office shall take the oath of office prescribed by the constitution of the state. The mayor of any of said cities shall designate one of such members to be the chairman of the parole commission of such city, and may, at the expiration of the term of the member appointed to hold office for two years, designate the member appointed for four years, or the member appointed for six years, or the member then appointed for a full ten year term, to be chairman of the parole commission of such city.

§ 2. This act shall take effect immediately.

STATE OF NEW YORK, }
Office of the Secretary of State, } ss:

I have compared the preceding with the original law on file in this office, and do hereby certify that the same is a correct transcript therefrom and of the whole of said original law.

FRANCIS M. HUGO,
Secretary of State.

www.ingramcontent.com/pod-product-compliance
Lightning Source LLC
LaVergne TN
LVHW011133110826
845150LV00008B/2320
9781418194680